CORNERSTONE

A Cluster of 21 Poems

Dr. Juliet Chand

BookLeaf
Publishing

India | USA | UK

Made with ❤ on the BookLeaf Publishing Platform
www.bookleafpub.in
www.bookleafpub.com

Dedication

"In the loving memory of my dear father the Late Mr. P.K.N Chand former Principal of St. Anthony Boy's School, Delhi, whose wisdom and warmth we will always cherish."

Preface

'Cornerstone' - A cluster of 21 heart touching poems is a thoughtful presentation of different perspectives and emotions. It's an attempt to bring before you a deep introspection within us. When we are in the gulf of sorrow there is always a hope that ignites us to come back from our setbacks.

I have been writing poems since I was a child and after graduation I was able to get some of them published in magazines too. But with my busy schedule I was unable to continue my desire of being a poet. But last year changed everything. I met with an accident and had multiple fractures in my right forearm. I was unable to write, do my household chores nor could manage my basic needs. I was so afraid of losing my job too.

For three months I had rigorous clinical visits to bring my forearm into functional condition. Writing anything became a challenge for me. I started composing poems and giving them a final shape took days as my scribbling on a piece of paper was my greatest achievement, an attempt to write perfectly.

Poetry has always been a passion for me. Whenever I am in distress I've found asylum in poems. It's a beautiful way to express feelings and emotions and I hope it will touch your hearts too. These poems are intellectual, motivational and religious that will awaken your spiritual journey as you sail smoothly in your life.

Acknowledgements

For the moments of quiet reflection, the words that flowed like a brook, and the unwavering belief in this journey, I offer my heartfelt gratitude to my dear mother and my sister for believing in me. With every poem, I also carry the echoes of those who encouraged me, kept motivating me and loved me through it all. This amazing cluster of 21 poems is for you.

1. MY GOLDEN WINGS
(A Story of a Butterfly)

Oh! Look at the colours I have,
The sublime texture that nature gives.
The beauty in itself to admire,
That I have in my golden wings.

Careless and carefree as I fly,
Dancing on every bud and flower.
Soaring high and low in the sky,
Making my way through the bower.

How pleasant was the breeze!
How sweet its fragrance is!
That lifted my spirit to accomplish
My dream in a trance.

Suddenly, from nowhere, dark clouds came,
The harsh breeze blew in rough terrain.
It blew me off to a tall mountain,
And broke my wings in vain.

Wounded, I fell on the ground,
My golden wings scattered all around.
No one to see, no one helped,

I cried to God and yelped.

He heard my cry and send angels down,
They found me helpless on the ground.
Wounded, bleed'd and in lot of pain,
Waiting for mercy in disdain.

The first angel stoop'd a little low,
Picked all my wings fallen below.
Then raising them all towards the sun,
And fixed them on me, one by one.

The second angel kept a careful watch,
As I moved my golden wings apart.
He gave me strength, that I gain,
To move my wings again and again.

I kept waiting what the third angel will flip,
He holds my wings to unlock its grip.
Lifted me up so that I could fly,
Blissful, I soar in the open sky.

Be grateful to God, who listens the meekest,
When you are in distress and pain.
Cry out to HIM with a great loud call,
His love and mercy is equal for all.

****

2. THE PERCEPTION

A girl in mess, speaks to you this day
'Once was proud to be what I am today.
Rejected all lies, fake and unrest.
Not to end my life, to live the toughest test.

Like dirt that covers diamond in dust,
My life is not cheap, to be lost in the crust.
Buried deep down is not my last wish.
To fight it back I just need to be quick.

Being intellectual or exceptional is only a perception,
The sole way out is your own selection.
The more you think, I'm more real than ever,
To surrender before dark clouds, I'll never.

I still hold the keys to resolve any query,
No matter the delay, solutions can be many.
Wisdom and courage both I possess,
Cast out your fear and follow what's correct.

Slowing down in life is full of jerks and bumps.
It's just a leap to step back for a huge jump.
Wrinkles on my face, dull eyes and dry lips,
Will never fade out the fighter within.

Troubles occur in everyone's life for sure,
Being a warrior you can tackle it far more.
The comebacks in life are true stepping stones,
Real me will bravely face all the turmoil alone.

The lesson I teach is both intellectual and exceptional,
With the growing age clarity comes with perception.
Don't die out the flame that burns in you,
Let your spark ignite the life of others too.

Wisdom shines on the face of the ones who delight,
From ash and dust will raise him back to life.
If you'll fight, do remain calm and still,
Your battles too will soon end up with a win.'

****

3. LAMENTATION OF A BROKEN TWIG

Lying on the ground, lament a broken twig
"As the days went by, I enjoyed the fig.
Holding the core of a branch, caring it tender leaves,
Nurturing the fruits it bore, beautiful sight to please."

"How happy I was, when I was in youth
Green leaves to admire, in mist peeping fruits.
The love I gave to them, flows through my veins,
All that I had I gave it for their gain."

I looked down at the broken twig,
Asked about its immense pain.
In agony she answered, "This pain is a bane,
From my life to my death, what did I gain?"

I console to the broken heart,
"To live a blissful life is truly an art.
What you gave no one can ever give,
The life you live no one can ever live."

"Don't lament on being a useless creature,
For once you were a part of this beautiful nature.
Your service to mankind, your duty was must,

You'll be remembered in all creations, I trust."

****

4. A WORD OF WISDOM THROUGH AN ANT

While lying on my bed, I happen to see
An ant crawling beside me.
Slowly it went by my sight,
Seeing its move was a complete delight.

I asked the ant - "What made you look tired?"
She replied,"The journey of my life that I hired.
My life has too many lessons to teach.
Are you ready to listen to them each?"

I wonder what a small ant has ensure
Lesson to teach that it implore,
"The journey I've walked is not new,
From ages we ants have been walking through.

The footsteps we take are without impression,
The wisdom received, we impart to future generations.
The kindness we share, the love we care,
The hope to meet, the message is sweet.

Work hard, the way you live is destined from above
Wisdom in knowing and keeping humanity above.
No one is great or small, in God's creation

Let's live peacefully as one nation."

****

5. THE WORD

In the fiery night of darkness,
A ray of hope flickers in the sky.
Swollen eyes filled with numbness,
To see Mercy at hand that lie.

Broken bones, stiff necks,
Sluggish liver and lungs pangs.
All suffered from ship reck,
Death howls with its fangs.

In the midst of sorrow's stream,
A word fell on this ear.
A light that shines across the beam,
I shut my eyes in dreadful fear.

Nearing death, I repent for sins,
Mercy bestowed on a helpless state.
Heavy voice I heard so dim,
What caused him to tremble and say.

"I've lost my ninety nine sheep,
You only stood for truth and faith.
I'll give the word - power to thee,
Bring them back to day Broadway."

"Life is more materialistic in many ways,
To mammon they sold their very soul.
Dissect genes to produce new race,
Nuclear arms is their new goal."

"Words fell on deaf ears,
So, pick your pen, I command.
God's spell are these you hear,
Listen with care, what I demand."

The words I wrote are His words,
Who directs me, is our Lord.
Insert in your heart, what you heard,
For these are the words of your Holy God.

****

6. OPUS – THE CREATION

Seeing his future insecure,
A boy in pain, hoping better in life,
With folded hands, he began to pray
To his maker above in dismay.

Plain was GOD'S canvas, he meditate
Darkness was all around.
To remove the darkness across,
He created the world round.

Day and night, HE created
And stretch'd HIS hand for skies.
Dry land for grass HE made,
For fish HE bound sea tides.

Sun, moon, stars HE stud forth,
To give light in the darkest night.
HE filled the whole earth with creatures,
In the sky, water and on earth, so bright.

Last but not the least, in HIS own image
He created the first man and woman.
To enjoy all HIS choicest blessings,
HE blessed them to be fruitful and one.

Then I heard a voice like a thunderbolt,
The true words that no one can hear.
Only for the choicest has the power,
To hear His voice so loud and clear.

"Don't be in dismay, my child," I say
"Don't be so troubled, my son.
From chaos I created the world in seven days,
Your life is just a simple one."

****

7. RAINBOW – A COVENANT WITH CREATION

Oh, look! The seven colours in the sky,
Beauty spread across the heavens so high.
These colours are his wonderful creation,
For I'll tell you of its first formation.

Men dwell and fill the earth,
In them sin swells fully by birth.
Every intent of thought was evil,
Forgetting God they worshipped devil.

He was sorry for His creation,
And thought to sweep all nations.
Beast and bird which he once embraced,
Has now put the Almighty in disgrace.

Only Noah found grace in His eyes,
He was saved and the rest were to die.
An ark was made with pitch and wood,
All the beasts and birds they kept were good.

Noah and his people, boarded the boat,

It protected the seeds as a strong fort.
The fountains of deeps were then broken,
The windows of Heaven were also open.

Forty days and Forty nights,
It rained all day and all night.
He swept every creature altogether,
As scribbling on board, erased for ever.

Only Noah and his people were to live,
A new life it was, what He gave.
Ark as twig, float'd on water,
Only He protected them from disaster.

Like a canary, it rested on Ararat,
A dove brought the message of love.
Water now abates from trees,
As a sign a leaf was in its beak.

All the saved seeds came out dried,
Thank'd the Lord, they weren't destroyed.
No flood will ever be the cause of destruction,
A rainbow was a sign of a covenant with creation.

Whenever you see a rainbow in the sky,
Just think of it for a while
He kept His promise, of destruction no more,

Let's promise Him truthfully, to sin no more.

****

8. HOPE IN REJECTION – CHRIST ALONE

The Spirit of the Lord is within me,
He gives words that I may speak.
Heals the one, who believe in thee,
While I preach good news to meek.

Then why is your deep faith flickering?
Have you lost your hope in Him?
How can doubt sleek into your thinking?
That trouble surrounds its rim.

His birth fulfilled the scriptures,
His deeds testify His coming.
His own people rejected His ventures,
Discouraging and totally rejecting.

The men on high seats hated Him though,
Not to follow His footsteps, like those
Who have risen from their loneliness,
And bow before Him in their meekness.

Even John confessed He is greater than him,
The One who comes from heaven's above .
They all did gather around him to listen,

To justify what they see and hear.

Scriptures alone can't give eternal life,
Follow in faith to regain his love.
Submit your spirit for a holy life,
Those who believe get eternal love.

He was not here to abolish law,
But He came to fulfill them all.
A new understanding He gave to the one
Who makes his way for His Holy Kingdom.

Their faith was less than a mustard seed,
So was criticised for what He said
He sits, eats and drinks with sinners,
These words were what sinners said.

His teachings was a pleasure to those,
Who hears, loves and enjoys His fellowship.
They rejoiced for their bridegroom in love,
So they longed for His companionship.

His teachings like old unshrunken cloth,
That couldn't be mend or replaced.
His words as new wine drench our thoughts,
Our deep soul is now well pleased.

9. VOICE IN THE WILDERNESS

"Oh! Great son of Zacharias, full of grace,
Your life on earth is just worthy of praise.
You're the chosen one of the Almighty God,
Bless'd is He who comes in the name of the LORD.

You cried in the wild to save us from sins,
Baptise in river water for our repentance.
You prepared the way for our Lord to come,
Straighten our paths for His glorious welcome.

Oh! Great son of Zacharias, so pious and humble,
What should I do to save myself?" I tremble.
"For the axe is now set to strike the root in spite,
Save me! Save me from His harsh smite."

"Turn to God," answered John,
"He is the One to save us from harm,
Cheat no more, desert no more,
Extortion on meek is no cure.

His powers you can't see but I can,
He's more powerful than I am.
Not worthy to open His sandal's strand,

Yet He'll baptise you with a mystical hand.

He'll carry His winnowing fork in hand,
To sieve and clear His threshing - land.
And will collect the good ones in His stock,
The chaff He'll put into an unquenchable flak."

Come LORD come, we've waited so long,
We looked for you and searched along.
Come LORD come, we pray and sing,
Come LORD come, we await for our KING.

****

10. A DONKEY'S PLEA

I.

'Standing by the river side,
Various images crossed my mind.
It's a Donkey's journey down the memory lane.
Of ancestral glory, he oft'n reminds.'

'I belong to that mighty family,
Whose ancestral deeds are recorded in pages.
I'm proud to be lofty and loyal.
To be of the same lineage.'

'I tell you a tale, of my great aunty,
She was oft'n known as Balaam's donkey.
The encounter she met with an unknown Messenger.
Saved her master's life, from His anger.'

II.

'The master rides, with serfs two beside,
Heading towards the city of Moab.
In a fit of fright, she turned aside,
Seeing the Messenger with the drawn sword.'

'He struck her, to turn to road,
The Messenger now stood in a narrow path.
To stop him further to rode,
She crushed his foot in order to halt.'

'Unseen Messenger stood still further narrow,
Leaving no space to move left or right.
Seeing fatal end in a great sorrow,
She lay down under her master's sight.'

'Struck her with staff in anger,
She rebelled against his cruel act.
Never she turned out as infallible,
She reminds him to think at his best.'

'Balaam's eyes were then open'd,
Almighty's Messenger stood against him.
Praised his donkey, who saved his life,
By now He would have slayed him.'

III.

'I'll tell you yet another, great aunt's niece,
Born with a purpose, to serve Lord's mother.
To serve our master, who spread peace,
She served more royally as ever.'

'She carried Most Pure, who bore Him,
And witnessed the birth of her first born son.
She served most loyally to them,
And was blessed with a cross over.'

'Since then we carry sign on our back,
For generations we'll carry it on.
With this sign no proud we lack,
For years we will carry it along.'

IV.

'That niece , sister had a great daughter,
She was young , with beauty as ever.
Her eyes were big as almonds seeds,
On whose back no one sat, never.'

'Our Lord saw her from Mount Olivet,
Asked two men to lose her ties.
Anyone asked, say Lord needs it,
As she served the most holy rites.'

'At once the cloaks were thrown at her back,
Made our Lord to sit on her as royal.
She walked as loyal as a mule could lack,
She gallantly entered, holy city of Israel.'

'Our Lord at back , wherever she step,
Cloaks were spread in honour to welcome,
In rejoice the gathering sang and clap,
For a king, in the name of Lord, has come.'

'I sing the tale of might and courage,
I carry the sign on my back.
I told the tale I heard from ages,
(At once she's load'd, four sand full sacks.)

V.

'I plead to mankind to have pity on me,
Remember the family that I too belong.
Load you put, is heavy you can see,
I cannot stand it for any long.'

'The sack is not full with sand,
I feel alone load'd with sin.
Nor such I found in any land,
That caused me so much pain.'

'Realised now how Christ felt,
While he carried a cross on His back.
My suffering is less, what He dwelt,
Why to worry about the weight that I had.'

****

11. ROSE - A PRECIOUS GIFT

One lonely night, at midnight hour,
Thrush awakes with a sudden quake.
Seeing bright light at a weary hour,
Aghast, what makes the Shepherds shake?

Rejoiced on hearing the message they spread,
The whole sky sings of His Glory and Name.
Shepherds decided to worship the child,
And offer the lamb, that was so tame.

Poor thrush had nothing to give,
Felt sorry for nothing she had.
She then decided, to sing for the Baby,
The precious thing she ever had.

Flew to the place where the Baby lay,
Perched high on a rose bush top.
View the Babe which sleeps on hay,
She jumped in joy and began to hop.

She sang and sang, with all her soul,
She sang as ever as she can,
With her full heart and mind whole,

She sang for the divine clan.

Not knowing the bush with thorns,
Carelessly she sat too close to one.
Truly drench'd in spirit of love,
It perched the little heart at once.

Not conscious of the sudden mishap,
She sang to the sleeping Babe, at low.
Blood gushed out and reach'd the bud,
That closed its eyes, of wind and snow.

She sang to her last breath, in bower,
Till her last drop, bloomed the rose.
A wind blew and carried the flower,
To our Lord's lovely little feet so close.

A precious gift a bird can ever give,
To the new born King of the whole nation.
More precious than gold, myrrh and frankincense,
Her voice, soul and flesh were her presentation.

****

12. A CHRISTMAS GIFT FOR ALL

Our Lord is born to this day,
Let's sing, be happy and gay.
End of all worries and sorrows within,
O come, let us adore Him.

Born between Heaven and Earth,
Blessed is His mother, blessed is His birth.
Blessed is the stable born within.
O come, let us adore Him.

Blessed is the night, blessed the day,
Blessed are the Angels that sing with gay.
All the joys we treasure within,
O come, let us adore Him.

Blessed are the shepherds, with sudden awake,
Feared the Angels, with fright they shake.
Celebrating jubilee they had within:
O come, let us adore Him.

Then came the Magi from distant land,
Following the star, that night at hand.
Seeing the Baby in manger within,

O come, let us adore Him.

Blessed is His Father, blessed is the Son,
Blessed is the Man, our hearts He has won.
Our hearts leap in joy here within.
O come, let us adore Him.

Blessed are you, unblessed is none,
Be blessed and rejoice ye everyone.
Our Redeemer is born, search within,
O come, let us adore Him.

****

13. THE HEM OF HIS GARMENT

The sun all set to blaze the sky in noon,
I'm in the midst of a crowd waiting.
Waiting for my chance, for my healing.
To see just his glimpse will be my boon,

In the midst of crowd my eyes to meet,
My healer kept me waiting so long.
Shrunk in the crowd alone,
Waiting for a chance to greet.

Someone please go and tell Him,
I am waiting from morning till eve.
Tell Him, that I'm here to seek,
My healing is only from Him.

In sweat I stand, in pain I weep,
Day to night I seek Him in town.
Aloof in crowd dropped myself down,
My healer stands in between to see.

Simply waiting, waiting and waiting ...

Like a creeper, I crept on the ground,

I dragged myself and crawled in pain.
Passing amidst the crowd again,
Looking for my saviour around.

Broken and shattered with my plea
Just only one touch is all I need,
The hem of His garment indeed,
Had made me whole and free.

The power, that touch rested on me,
My master turned to me and said —
'You are healed of your sorrows and pain.'
Go and thank the Almighty for the same.

The light that healed this sick dame,
Redeemer redeemed, from bondage and sin,
Forgiving all sinners and making me akin.
Blessed is His Holy Name!

My healer took my just heed,
My life is now fully won,
You too can be the one,
This divine touch is all you need.

JUST ONE TOUCH IS ALL YOU NEED!

****

14. VICTORY OVER DEATH

I.

In the early hours of the day,
In the garden stood Mary weeping.
Peeping in the tomb, where they lay,
Her dead master, so peace loving.

She saw two angels in white,
They sat in the tomb on either side.
To query her for what she cried,
She humbly stood there beside,

"What made you Mary to weep,
What causes your eyes to swell?
Sorrow you've root'd so deep,
That caused your heart in pain to dwell?"

II .

"I'm looking for my dead Master,
This's His Third day, where does He lay?
I've not seen His body there after,
Since I visited Him yesterday?

Unjustly judged at Pontius Pilate's hand,
Wiped, spitted and suffered humiliation
To be nailed and crossed at Golgotha's land,
Cruel, I'll - treated him till culmination."

Died at the cross, our sins he took,
We've lost our dear Saviour.
The whole earth in tremble shook.
Tore the temple's veil of interior."

III .

She turned back and saw a man,
Not realising to be the Son of God.
She pleaded him to return the man,
To take Him back, her dear Lord.

He reveal'd Himself to her,
To make her realise that He's living.
To tell everyone out there,
And spread the message that He's giving.

Go to my brethren, and tell,
"I'm ascending to my Father and yours.
Go to Galilee as well.
Surely they'll meet the Lord in hours."

IV .

For Death is swallowed by Victory,
There are no more its stings.
Hades defeat, now records in history,
Out of death came life as Spring.

With The First Man came death,
Though he was made to live.
The last Man came with spirit,
And gave eternal life in bliss.

Then let us celebrate His resurrection,
For no more we're dead but alive.
Now there'll be no fear of destruction,
As our Saviour stands by our side.

****

15. GOD'S HAND IN EVERYTHING

When you see the nature around,
A gentle breeze kissing the ground.
The artistic hues in every being, then
It's God's Hand in everything.

When a bud blooms to a beautiful flower,
And sweet smelling trees in the bower.
The birds flying high with open wings, then
It's God's Hand in everything.

When you wake up at sun rise,
And beauty spread across the skies
Colourful beams floats in clouds string, then
It's God's Hand in everything.

When dry earth cries for rain,
And clear water dries up again.
Deep inside water gushes as spring, then
It's God's Hand in everything.

When the rain quenches thirsty crust,
And seedling springs burst.
A plant forms out of sapling, then

It's God's Hand in everything.

When dark clouds cover the sky,
And a thunder storm makes you cry.
Sudden commotion calms deep within, then
It's God's Hand in everything.

When you see a bird nest,
And you care for it along its crest.
The flight of the bird, the joy it brings, then
It's God's Hand in everything.

When you make a child smile,
And you walk with him for a while.
The happiness across his cheeks it bring, then
It's God's Hand in everything.

When you care for the meek, needy and old,
And turn their lives more precious than gold.
The life you give beyond The spring, then
It's God's Hand in everything.

When we humans believe in faith,
And raise our voices for His grace.
Showers of love that flings, then
It's God's Hand in everything.

****

16. MY VISION – MY NEW WORLD

My wonder vision of the world,
How beautiful it will be!
All intellect and leaders of the world,
Bring new rising in their lead.

How develop the new world will be
A new politics in action to see!

My wonder vision of the world,
How just, it will be!
No difference in mankind,
Social equality in the world, to see.

How social the world will be,
For a new horizon it will glean!

My wonder vision of the world,
How stable it will be!
Every man will hold a share,
A new entrepreneur he will be.

How wealthy the world will be
In the new economy it will gleam!

I wonder how wonderful it will be!
To see the world connecting visually.
This vision may never remain just a vision.
Uniting the world as a big nation.

My vision of a narrower world,
In horizon, a world by intellect to be.

Let the Creator, create a new world,
In peace and harmony may all live.
Both mighty and meek may dwell
Together, in the world of peaceful beings.

How beautiful the world will be,
Created by the Creator, to see!

****

17. YES I CAN READ
(Queries of a small child)

"Teacher, what is it
That spelt like this — r.i.v.e.r"

"The water you see,
That move around the trees
And nourishes the Earth.
The word that you read
Is a river indeed."

"Yes I can read."

"Teacher, what is it
That spelt like this — f.i.r.e"

"The wood that you see,
It comes from the tree,
On which your mother cook food
Is fire indeed."

"Yes, I can read."

"Teacher, what is it
That spelt like this — e.a.r.t.h."

"The home of all creature,
It is the seat of mother nature.
Life giver, protector and destroyer.
All three it comprises in dearth,
Is indeed our planet earth."

"Yes. I can read."

"Teacher, what is it
That spelt like this — r.a.i.n."

"That quenches the thirst of crops,
That sprouts the dead seed up.
Farmers longs and wait for it.
Indeed drops of rain it is."

"Yes, I can read."

"Teacher, what it is like,
When I read you always delight.
It spelt like this — w.o.r.d.
Teacher, please tell me what it means."

"It's the world of knowledge and wisdom,
It's the source of intellect and light.
It's the beginning of discoveries and inventions,

On it the whole world pride,
Indeed it is the word, I delight."

"Yes, I can read."

"Teacher, who is he
When you see Him, you always bow.
It's spelt this way – G.O.D
Is he really bigger than you and me?"

"The world you are in, He made
Alpha and Omega is He,
He runs the whole world in His stride,
He is surely bigger than you and me.
Almighty God, He is indeed."

"Yes. I too can say
I can read."

****

18. AN ODE TO THE SCREEN LOVERS

O Dear ones! How busy you are!
Drowned in the bright screen this late hour.
Lost in your own world of digital amaze,
To just scroll and click this artificial blaze.

How I long you to see nature's plight,
Between the trees peep the bright sunlight.
Lift up your eyes and gaze at its beauty,
To treasure it all, is your first duty.

The happy family hours, you spend together,
Are no more but lost and gone forever.
Your screen, your cage, a fake delight,
It stole all the joy of days and nights.

Once you were a part of this beautiful creation,
O soulful mind! Full of compassion.
Now your time passes by gazing at the screen.
That you forget your meals and sleep, I mean.

Your eyes have blur, your mind is captive,
Your own device has made you inactive.
Once you mastered it, all alone,

Has made you his slave and lone.

Listen to me, O dear screen lover!
Break those chains of digital power.
Behold peace! In the midst of God's creation,
Save yourself from on screen temptation.

****

19. Friendship - A Bond Forever

I want a friend to the very end,
To sing, eat and dance together.
I want a friend for a happy end.
That will last long forever.

I need a friend, a close one,
Who can weep and laugh together.
I need a friend a pure one,
I don't want anything beside her.

I wish for a friend so dear to me,
That can walk and talk for miles.
I wish a friend to the very end,
For me, more precious is her smiles.

I long for a friend much like me,
With whom I can share all that I have.
A gift of God is my dear friend,
No one else I want beside that.

****

20. MY LADY — MY TREASURE

I don't know for what I see in her,
Simple, humble, loveable for sure.
I see my lady, more precious than jewel,
She's more beautiful than gold.

My heart longs for her,
I trust her more and more.
Fully compassionate and contended
She lacks nothing for sure.

Early she rise, while others still in bed,
Provides food for all, I cherish much.
Laying hands on things, ahead,
She brings more profits, in a bunch.

From winter snow to heated summer,
Her hands stitch clothes for all.
Fine linen she spins all day,
Beautiful garments with great length fall.

Her magic is pure, no fault I see,
She keeps her house in order.
From eldest son to youngest daughter,

All praise is only for her.

Seen many ladies, that I came across
You're the best from all.
No deceit, no cheat, no laziness,
In your wisdom rest for sure.

The love you show, no one else has
Your beauty are your deeds and works.
The blessings of GOD, that you have
My love, you are the most worthy one.

****

21. A TRIBUTE

****

A TRIBUTE TO MY DEAR FATHER

FROM MY BIRTH TO THIS DAY
SINCE CHILDHOOD TILL TODAY
UNDER WHOSE PROTECTION, GUIDANCE AND
CARE
ALL MY WORRIES ARE FAR TO BARE
MY GUIDE, TEACHER ALL IS HE
SUPPORTER AND CARETAKER WHO CAN BE
BY WHOSE POWER AND HIS FAME
I CAN NEITHER STAND NOR MY NAME
MY MORALS AND ATTRIBUTES ARE MY BEAUTY
TO WORK HARD IS MY FIRST DUTY
TO THE GREAT HEIGHTS HIS GLORY MAY SHINE
TO ME HE IS NOT ONLY MORTAL BUT DIVINE
NO PERSON CAN BE AS INTELLIGENT AS HE
NO PERSON CAN BE AS GENEROUS AS HE
OFTEN HE SEEMS TO BE BOLD RATHER
BUT HE WILL ALWAYS BE MY DEAR FATHER

****

www.ingramcontent.com/pod-product-compliance
Lightning Source LLC
Chambersburg PA
CBHW070457050426
42449CB00012B/3017